CORNERSTONES OF FREEDOM™

W9-CAV-797

ROMNEY VS. OBAMA: ELECTION 2012

BY PETER BENOIT

CHILDREN'S PRESS®

An Imprint of Scholastic Inc.
New York   Toronto   London   Auckland   Sydney
Mexico City   New Delhi   Hong Kong
Danbury, Connecticut

BRINGING HISTORY to LIFE

Content Consultant: James Marten, PhD
Professor and Chair, History Department
Marquette University, Milwaukee, Wisconsin

Cataloging-in-Publication data is available from the Library of Congress

ISBN-13: 978-0-531-22499-1 (pbk)

All rights reserved. Published in 2013 by Children's Press, an imprint of
Scholastic Inc.
Printed in the United States of America 113

1 2 3 4 5 6 7 8 9 10 R 22 21 20 19 18 17 16 15 14 13

Photographs © 2013: Alamy Images: 8 (Kristoffer Tripplaar), 30 (Richard Levine);
AP Images: 5 top, 36 (Charles Dharapak), 41 (Franklin Reyes), 21 (Jim Rogash),
cover (Kevin Sanders), 14 (Kevork Djansezian), 40 (Kyodo), 23, 57 top (Mark
Terrill), 18 (North Wind Picture Archives), 10 (Obama Presidential Campaign),
29 (Pablo Martinez Monsivais), 5 bottom, 14, 32, 57 bottom (Rex Features), 51
bottom (Sipa), 19; Dreamstime/Leach: cover background; Getty Images: 13, 20
(Boston Globe), 54 (Jeff J Mitchell), 42 (JEWEL SAMAD/AFP), 51 top (Stephen
Ferry); Landov: 33 (Larry Downing/Reuters), 12 (Obama Press Office/UPI), 27
(Tami Chappell/Reuters); PhotoEdit/A. Ramey: 37; Shutterstock, Inc./Orhan
Cam: 4 bottom, 6; Superstock, Inc.: 45 (age fotostock), 46, 56 (Culver Pictures,
Ind), 44 (Dream Pictures/Blend Images), 48 (Everett Collection), 38 (Science
Faction), 43 (Ton Koene/age fotostock); The Image Works: 49 (akg-images), 55
(Andrew Lichtenstein), 26 (Bob Daemmrich), 2, 3, 7, 16 (Christopher Fitzgerald/
CandidatePhotos), 35 (Marjorie Kamys Cotera/Daemmrich Photos), 24 (Michael
Geissinger); U.S. Navy/Mass Communication Specialist 3rd Class Michael Croft:
cover, back cover.

Maps by XNR Productions, Inc.

Did you know that studying history can be fun?

BRING HISTORY TO LIFE by becoming a history investigator. Examine the evidence (primary and secondary source materials); cross-examine the people and witnesses. Take a look at what was happening at the time—but be careful! What happened years ago might suddenly become incredibly interesting and change the way you think!

Contents

An Important Decision

The office of president is the highest position in the United States government.

On Tuesday, November 6, 2012, voters across the United States will go to the polls to elect the next president of the United States. Voting is both a responsibility and a privilege. The candidate elected in November will play an important role in shaping America's image abroad, as often happens during times of military conflicts. The new president may face crises that test his resolve, as John F. Kennedy did after winning the 1960 election. He will be asked to steer the nation's struggling **economy** into calm waters, just as Franklin D. Roosevelt was when voters elected him in 1932.

This time, voters will decide whether Democratic president Barack Obama or Republican challenger Mitt Romney is better able to meet the demands of the times. Which one will be able to guide the nation's economy, set its immigration laws, and protect it from terrorism? Obama and Romney stand in stark contrast to each other, with different backgrounds, political beliefs, and **platforms**. Voters are equally divided in their own vision of America's future and its role in the world. They will choose the candidate whose views most closely match their own. Their choice on November 6 will shape the world. Let's meet the candidates.

Voters will choose between Barack Obama and Mitt Romney when they go to the polls to vote on November 6, 2012.

ESIDENT TO LIVE IN THE WHITE HOUSE.

CHAPTER 1

BARACK OBAMA

Barack Obama is the 44th president of the United States.

BARACK OBAMA WAS BORN ON
August 4, 1961, in Honolulu, Hawaii. His mother
and father had met the previous year as students
in a Russian language class at the University of
Hawaii. They got married less than a year later.
The two came from different worlds. Barack
Obama Sr. was from Kenya. He had come to
America after receiving a scholarship to study
economics. Stanley Ann Dunham was born in
Wichita, Kansas. Her family moved to Washington
State when she was a girl. They lived there for
several years before moving to Hawaii.

Barack Obama grew up in Hawaii and Indonesia.

Obama Sr. won a scholarship to Harvard University after finishing his studies in Hawaii in 1963. He left his wife and young son behind as he traveled to Massachusetts to attend school. Stanley Ann resumed her studies in Hawaii and divorced her husband. In 1966, she married Lolo Soetoro, a graduate student in geography at the University of Hawaii. Stanley Ann and young Barack accompanied him when he returned to his native Indonesia a year later.

Barack attended school in Jakarta, Indonesia, until he was 10. He was first enrolled at the St. Francis of Assisi School, then studied for two years at the prestigious Besuki School. The Besuki School instilled high academic standards in young Barack. It also brought him together with people of diverse faiths and backgrounds. Then, in 1971, 10-year-old Barack moved back to Hawaii, where he lived with his grandparents and attended the academically challenging Punahou School.

Obama's high school friends at Punahou School remember him as popular and intelligent. They saw no hint of his political future, though he excelled in debate. After graduation, he headed to Occidental College in Los Angeles, California. There, his political activism began to emerge. Near the end of his two years at Occidental, he became involved in campus protests against **apartheid**. He and his fellow protesters urged the college to apply economic pressure to South Africa by withdrawing investments. In 1981, Obama transferred to Columbia University in New York City. He pursued studies in political science with newfound passion and graduated in 1983. Obama spent the next two years working in New York, first as a financial writer and then as part of a civil rights organization.

Making an Impact

Obama's life shifted direction again in 1985. He moved to Chicago and worked as a community organizer on Chicago's South Side. He opened an office that helped the city's poor find jobs. He also organized neighborhood watch groups. These groups empowered residents to keep a lookout for criminal activities in their neighborhoods. He made Altgeld Gardens, a mostly African American housing project, a safer place to live in by helping to have **asbestos** removed from the buildings. After three years of this work, he realized he could have a greater impact as a lawyer. He enrolled at Harvard Law School and started classes in 1988.

Obama excelled in law school. He became an editor of the prestigious *Harvard Law Review* at the end of his first year. The following year, he became the first black president of the publication. In 1991, he appeared in a "Black History Minute" segment on TBS, recalling the great civil rights

Obama poses with his grandparents in New York City during his time as a student at Columbia University.

Barack Obama made history as the first African American president of the *Harvard Law Review*.

lawyer Charles Hamilton Houston. Obama returned to Chicago after graduating later that year.

He quickly made his influence felt in Chicago. Realizing that minorities and low-income voters are often underrepresented, he took the lead in Chicago's voter registration drive. Obama taught constitutional law at the University of Chicago Law School from 1992 to 2004. He also served as an attorney for a firm specializing in civil rights cases and economic development in minority neighborhoods.

A stirring speech at the 2004 Democratic National Convention brought Obama national fame.

Obama was elected to the state senate in 1996 and served Illinois's 13th District until 2004. By 2002, he had become a vocal critic of President George W. Bush and the Iraq War. In his keynote address at the 2004 Democratic National Convention, he criticized President Bush while stressing the unity of the American people. A few months later, he won a U.S. Senate seat in a landslide election. The media and political insiders began to weigh his future as a presidential candidate.

Barack Obama won the Democratic nomination for the 2008 presidential election. On November 4, he was victorious in the general election. Obama faced immediate challenges that defined his time as president. The U.S. economy was in the middle of a **recession** when he took office. He addressed this issue by supporting economic stimulus packages in 2009 and 2010. He also took office as the country's military was fighting wars in Iraq and Afghanistan. President Obama ended the Iraq War. However, he increased U.S. troop strength in Afghanistan. There were few quiet moments during these years in office.

SPOTLIGHT ON

Michelle Obama

Michelle Robinson Obama was born in 1964. She grew up on Chicago's South Side. After graduating from Harvard Law School, she returned to her home city to work at the Sidley Austin law firm. There, she met Barack Obama. He was a summer intern at the firm, and Michelle was his adviser. The two soon began dating and were married in October 1992.

Michelle has held a number of positions in Chicago's city government. She was at first reluctant to campaign in her husband's bids for political office, but soon became his strongest supporter. Michelle Obama has become a role model for women. As First Lady, she works to promote nutrition and supports the president's economic policies.

CHAPTER 2

MITT ROMNEY

The 2012 election is Mitt Romney's second attempt to become president.

WILLARD MITT ROMNEY WAS

born on March 12, 1947, in Detroit, Michigan.
He was the fourth child of George and Lenore
Romney. George Romney was an influential
leader in the automotive industry. During World
War II, he played a key role in coordinating the
industry's contribution to the war effort. By 1954,
he was president of American Motors. His son Mitt
admired these achievements.

Young Mitt Romney led a privileged life. Though
he began his education in the public schools, he
was enrolled in an elite prep school when he was in
seventh grade. His friends remember him as a good
student and athlete.

YESTERDAY'S HEADLINES

Mitt Romney's family has long followed the Mormon religion. His great-great-grandfather, Parley Pratt, was among the religion's first members. In the early years of the Mormon faith, anti-Mormon feelings were common. Founder Joseph Smith (above) was the founder of the Mormon religion. Many Mormon beliefs opposed the ideas about religion that most people in the United States held at the time. Mormons were also looked down upon for continuing to practice **polygamy**, which the Mormon church had officially renounced in 1890.

Many people still criticize Mormons for some of their religious beliefs. Religion will be a major factor in the 2012 election.

During his sophomore year of high school, Mitt helped in his father's successful campaign to become governor of Michigan. By his senior year, he had gotten to know Ann Davies, the woman he would later marry.

Mitt went to Stanford University after he graduated from high school. After one year, he left for France to serve as a Mormon **missionary** for two and a half years. The French did not appreciate Romney and the other missionaries because their religion and cultural beliefs were too different from those of the French. Day after day, 19-year-old Mitt went door-to-door seeking converts. He was rejected over and over again. However, his own faith began to grow deeper.

By early 1968, Romney was assisting Paris mission president H. Duane Anderson. Then disaster struck. Romney, Anderson, and others were in a terrible car accident. Anderson was injured and his wife was killed. Romney was called upon to assume leadership of the mission while Anderson recovered.

When Romney returned home at the end of his mission, he resumed his college studies at Brigham Young University. He took time to help with his mother's unsuccessful bid for a U.S. Senate seat, and he married Ann Davies. He also became a dedicated student and

Mitt Romney (right) greatly admired his father, Michigan governor George Romney (left).

graduated with the highest honors. Wishing to follow his father's path, he went on to earn business and law degrees at Harvard.

A Life's Work

Romney's education prepared him to work for Bain & Company in Boston, Massachusetts. Bain worked closely with other businesses to help them improve their performance. Romney's work ethic and talent carried him to a leadership position within a few years. In 1984, he left to become a partner in a spin-off company called Bain Capital. Romney grew wealthy by leading the company as it bought and sold other companies. Bain Capital invested in well-known companies such as Staples, Domino's Pizza, and Sports Authority.

Romney's success as the leader of Bain Capital made him incredibly wealthy.

Romney was unable to defeat Edward M. Kennedy in his 1994 U.S. Senate campaign.

At the same time, Romney assumed a leadership role in the Mormon church in Massachusetts. He helped with the church's educational efforts and developed personal relationships with recently converted members.

His commitment to the people of his church was a turning point for him. His thoughts increasingly turned to entering politics. In 1994, he ran unsuccessfully against **incumbent** U.S. senator Edward M. Kennedy. By 2002, he was looking for a new direction. He had amassed a considerable fortune and was ready for new challenges.

His talents in financial management caught the attention of the struggling Salt Lake City Winter Olympics. Under Romney's direction, the Olympics in Utah were a financial success.

A VIEW FROM ABROAD

The 2002 Salt Lake City Olympics were the first Olympic Games held after the terrorist attacks of September 11, 2001. Many people worried that terrorists might attack the huge crowds that would be at the games. Enormous amounts of money were spent on security to put to rest the concerns of the participating athletes. This drove the Olympics into record debt. When Mitt Romney took over leadership of the games, he **lobbied** Congress to bail out the Salt Lake City Olympics. The government agreed to spend about $1.3 billion rescuing the games.

Romney's lobbying efforts may come back to haunt him in the 2012 election. He was very critical of President Obama's support of using government money to bail out private businesses during the recession. Critics point out that this was not much different than what Romney had done during the Olympics.

That success propelled Romney to victory in the 2002 Massachusetts **gubernatorial** election. During his one term as governor of Massachusetts, Romney cut spending and brought health care to almost all Massachusetts residents. He decided not to seek a second term so that he could campaign full time for the Republican nomination in the 2008 presidential election. However, he lost the nomination to John McCain.

Mitt Romney's political views have evolved with his ambition. He has gradually become more **conservative** in his outlook. As a result, the choice in November 2012 will be clearer for many voters. The candidates have very different ideas and backgrounds. The campaign will be hard fought and expensive. There is certain to be negative campaigning, and the battle for undecided votes will be fierce.

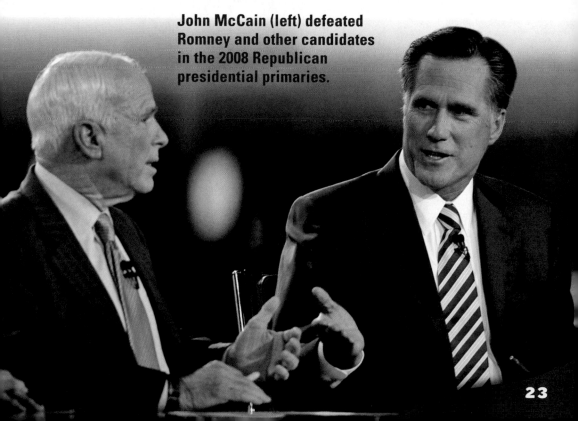

John McCain (left) defeated Romney and other candidates in the 2008 Republican presidential primaries.

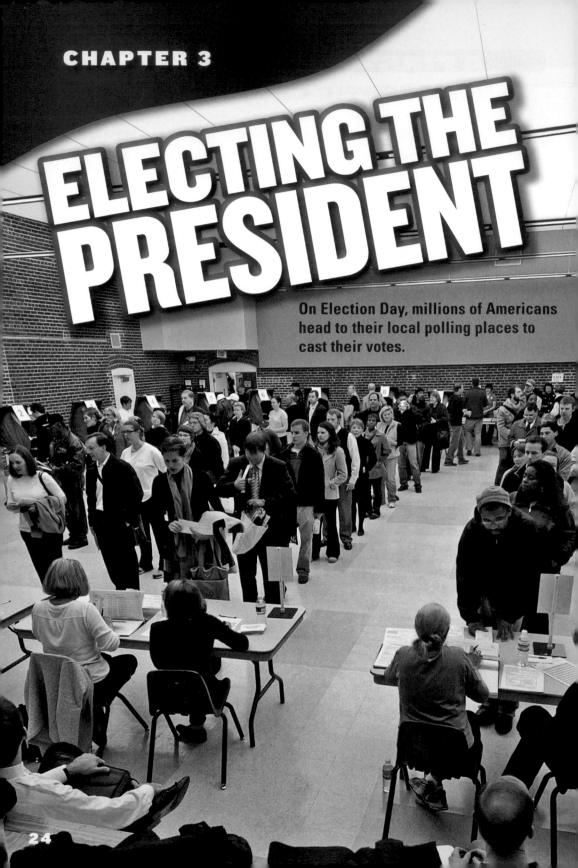

CHAPTER 3

ELECTING THE PRESIDENT

On Election Day, millions of Americans head to their local polling places to cast their votes.

WHEN VOTERS GO TO THE polls in November, they cast ballots for the candidate they prefer. But voters do not directly elect the president. That task belongs to 538 electors chosen by state **legislatures**. Voters are actually choosing electors. Each state has a number of electors equal to its congressional representation. Washington, D.C., has three electors. In most states, the candidate receiving the most popular votes gets all of that state's electoral votes. Other states split their electoral votes, with electors from each congressional district voting for the candidate receiving the most popular votes in that district. Electors will cast their votes in December at their respective state capitals. The results are read before Congress in early January, finalizing the election.

Many Americans want to change the way the president is elected. They point out that there is little to keep electors from going against the public polling results and choosing the other candidate. Such situations are very rare, however. Opponents of electoral voting would like to see it replaced with a nationwide popular vote.

Because of the way the system currently works, the winner of the popular vote does not always win the election. In the 2000 presidential election, Democrat Al Gore received more popular votes than Republican George W. Bush. However, Bush won the presidency with 271 electoral votes. A minimum of 270 electoral votes is required to win.

Members of each state's electoral college cast the votes that determine a presidential election.

If a large state has voted either Democrat or Republican in all recent elections, candidates are less likely to campaign there, believing that the state's electoral votes are already decided. Instead, they focus most of their attention on larger states where preferences are less clear-cut.

The Battle for the Presidency

Political campaigning is not merely a matter of informing voters what a candidate will do for them. Candidates have always known that raising questions about an opponent may turn votes their

YESTERDAY'S HEADLINES

The 2000 presidential election eventually saw Republican George W. Bush prevail over Democrat Al Gore. In the wee hours of the morning following Election Day, the results hinged on the popular vote in a few districts in Florida. Bush was declared the state's winner by just a few votes. However, many people believed that the votes were counted unfairly. A recount was eventually ordered, but the results were disputed. The outcome divided the nation. The matter dragged on for more than a month until the Supreme Court intervened and settled in favor of Bush. Gore had won the popular vote yet lost the election.

way. Negative campaigning stirs a variety of emotions in voters. Generally, attacks against an opponent that don't relate directly to his or her ability to perform duties in office are considered unfair. On the other hand, negative campaigning that addresses issues of character is considered fair. Attacks on issues of policy are generally always fair.

Negative campaigning has been part of the 2012 race as well, and the two candidates have walked a fine line between swaying voters and offending them. Negative campaigning will not end after this election. It will continue because history has shown that it works. Whether positive or negative, political campaigning through the media and the Internet will shape voters' ideas to a greater extent than ever before.

Campaign funding has been different in 2012. A Supreme Court decision in 2010 legalized unlimited campaign contributions but declared it illegal for supporters to coordinate directly with candidates. As

A FIRSTHAND LOOK AT
THE DAISY AD

On September 7, 1964, President Lyndon Johnson's reelection campaign aired an advertisement attacking opponent Barry Goldwater. It took advantage of public fear of nuclear weapons and the possibility that Goldwater might use them in Vietnam. The ad is still considered one of the most extreme examples of negative campaigning. See page 60 for a link to view the ad online.

a result, wealthy individuals and organizations are allowed to spend enormous amounts of money campaigning for their preferred candidates. Large, well-funded groups called super PACs (political action committees) have arisen as a result of this change in the law. Super PACs are not officially associated with specific candidates, but they spend tens of millions of dollars on campaign advertisements. Critics have complained that these groups give unfair power to wealthy people and corporations when it comes to getting the word out about candidates.

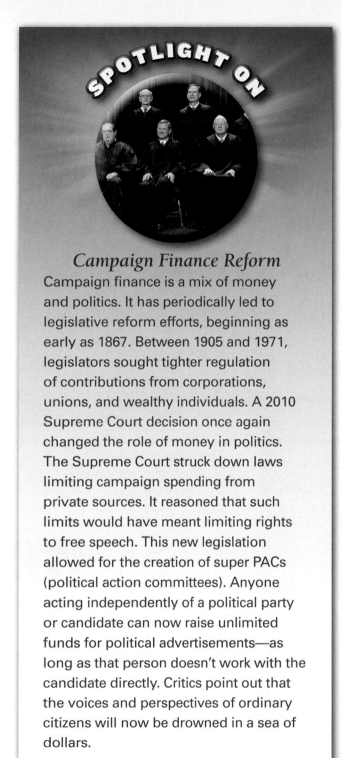

SPOTLIGHT ON

Campaign Finance Reform

Campaign finance is a mix of money and politics. It has periodically led to legislative reform efforts, beginning as early as 1867. Between 1905 and 1971, legislators sought tighter regulation of contributions from corporations, unions, and wealthy individuals. A 2010 Supreme Court decision once again changed the role of money in politics. The Supreme Court struck down laws limiting campaign spending from private sources. It reasoned that such limits would have meant limiting rights to free speech. This new legislation allowed for the creation of super PACs (political action committees). Anyone acting independently of a political party or candidate can now raise unlimited funds for political advertisements—as long as that person doesn't work with the candidate directly. Critics point out that the voices and perspectives of ordinary citizens will now be drowned in a sea of dollars.

CHAPTER 4

AMERICA AT THE CROSSROADS

Since the recession of 2008, many Americans have had trouble finding work.

WHERE ARE THE JOBS?

More jobs need to be created, and sooner. More jobs for older workers. No more age discrimination. No more credit background checks.

INFORMED VOTERS WILL MAKE their decisions based on key issues facing the nation both at home and abroad. The economy is central to the debate. Immigration, education, and the budget will also play decisive parts in the outcome of the election. Where do the candidates stand on these issues?

President Obama has worked hard to restore the country's economy in the wake of the recession.

Unemployment, Recession, Budget, and the Election

The election is expected to focus heavily on the state of the nation's struggling economy. Election 2012 will be, in part, a vote for or against President Obama's economic programs. An improvement in the economy in the months leading up to the election could swing the outcome in his favor. Obama has supported a combination of economic stimulus, lending, and bailouts to prevent the collapse of the economy.

Some economists agree with President Obama that these measures helped the nation avoid even worse economic disaster. They point to job creation and declines in the unemployment rate as indicators of an improving economy.

Obama also wants to address other factors that have made economic recovery difficult. For example, new technologies have made some jobs obsolete. If reelected, he plans to repeal tax cuts put in place by President George W. Bush and to work to reduce unemployment further. He believes that combining these changes with reduced government and military spending will bring significant improvements to the U.S. economy.

TODAY'S PERSPECTIVE

President Obama announced his first stimulus package, the American Recovery and Reinvestment Act, in 2009. Many Americans imagined it would create jobs, rebuild the nation's deteriorating bridges and roadways, and lift the country out of the recession. But not everyone was happy with the results of the act. Some critics see it as a failure, which they blame on fraud and corruption. They claim that more than half of the money was diverted into other plans and that unemployment rates did not drop as much as they should have. Others believe that the act prevented the nation's economy from becoming even worse. The outcome of the American Recovery and Reinvestment Act will be a major issue in the 2012 election.

Challenger Mitt Romney takes a different approach. He has put forward a plan with 59 specific proposals. Ten of them would be enacted on his first day as president. He plans to cut taxes in an attempt to grow the economy and create jobs. Specifically, he hopes to immediately reduce the corporate income tax rate. Like many conservative politicians, he believes that businesses will spend more money on research and employment if they do not have to spend as much on taxes. In addition, he would cut federal spending to balance the budget. Candidate Romney has also said he will work to reduce reliance on foreign oil by cutting the time it takes U.S. energy companies to get an oil drilling permit.

Immigration

In recent years, immigration has been an important issue for many Americans. Mitt Romney draws a sharp distinction between legal and illegal immigration. He points out that legal immigration "brings us education, new cultures, ideas, [and] innovative talent." However, he stands strong against illegal immigration. He has said that state and local authorities must become more involved in upholding immigration laws. He is strongly against the idea of allowing current illegal immigrants to remain in the United States. He is also in favor of completing construction of the U.S.-Mexico border fence.

President Obama points out that federal authorities already claim that the number of illegal crossings on the U.S.-Mexico border is decreasing. He has said that it would be impossible to find and deport the more than 10 million illegal immigrants. Many of them work, and their children have grown up in the United States. Obama speaks of the "pain and heartbreak" of deportation

After becoming citizens, immigrants enjoy the same rights as those who have lived in the country since birth.

and its toll on families. In June 2012, President Obama announced a new immigration policy. It will allow illegal immigrants who have been in the United States since they were children to stay in the country as long as they either finish high school or join the military. Obama realizes that immigration laws, however flawed, must be reinforced. In a July 1, 2010, speech, Obama stressed that illegal immigrants "should be required to register, pay their taxes, pay a fine, and learn English." He does not favor increasing U.S. Border Patrol above current levels or completing the border fence.

Each candidate has a plan for improving the nation's education system.

Education

Education is another topic that many Americans are concerned about today. The candidates' education policies differ in some aspects, but are similar in others.

Barack Obama has suggested putting $10 billion into early education. He also supports summer learning programs for children from disadvantaged backgrounds. He believes schools that do not perform well need support rather than punishment.

Mitt Romney stresses the importance of getting parents involved in education. He also proposes raising teacher salaries to attract better teachers. Additionally, he believes schools should be able to replace teachers who consistently perform poorly. To teach children the importance of understanding economics, he supports educating them on the topic starting at an early age.

SPOTLIGHT ON

U.S.-Mexico Border Fence

The U.S.-Mexico border fence is a sequence of separation barriers along the border between the United States and Mexico. It was put up in response to illegal immigration and the danger of terrorist threats. The fence has lessened illegal crossings from Mexico somewhat, but it has not been effective overall.

The fence has been controversial for several reasons. Opponents claim it causes environmental damage. It also cuts across and divides protected Native American lands. The project became extremely expensive. This made it especially unpopular in a struggling economy. Still, many Americans are in favor of the border fence.

CHAPTER 5

VOTERS WILL SHAPE YOUR WORLD

The War in Afghanistan is a controversial issue among many Americans.

THE ECONOMY AND

unemployment are widely considered to be the most pressing issues in the 2012 election. However, foreign policy issues increasingly occupy the minds of voters. They worry about the emerging nuclear capabilities of Iran and North Korea, as well as America's role in Afghanistan. The candidates vary sharply in their approaches to the growth of China's economic power. They also have very different priorities in addressing the problem of climate change.

North Korean leader Kim Jong-un has continued his country's nuclear weapons program since coming to power in 2011.

Nuclear Threats

North Korea has been unwilling to permit International Atomic Energy Agency inspectors to examine its nuclear facilities. Romney suggests that this sends a frightening signal to the world. Both candidates are alarmed by missile tests that raise the risk of a nuclear strike, as well as North Korea's sale of missile technology to Iran. Romney favors a firm approach to North Korea. President Obama points out that North Korea has failed to honor prior commitments to the international community. He favors further economic punishments against that country.

A FIRSTHAND LOOK AT
THE ESFAHAN NUCLEAR SITE

Reports of an explosion near the Esfahan Nuclear Site began to come out of Iran on November 28, 2011. Investigators thought they might have their first substantial proof of an Iranian nuclear weapons program. Satellite images of the site give no clear indication of an explosion. See page 60 for a link to view the nuclear site online.

Iran is believed to be making nuclear weapons of its own. Iranian president Mahmoud Ahmadinejad has repeatedly insisted that his country's nuclear program does not produce nuclear weapons. Obama has suggested a diplomatic approach to ease tensions

Mahmoud Ahmadinejad has been the president of Iran since 2005.

President Obama has sought to find common ground with Chinese president Hu Jintao and other Chinese leaders.

and find points of common interest. Mitt Romney has condemned the president's stance on Iran. In a January 2012 appearance in New Hampshire, he outlined a plan calling for trade restrictions and support of those fighting against Iran's ruling party. He feels that the United States must act decisively or risk Iran becoming a dangerous nuclear power.

China and Afghanistan

President Obama has hailed the emergence of China as a world power. He points out that China and the United

States have common interests in stabilizing Afghanistan and limiting North Korea's nuclear program.

Romney's position differs sharply from Obama's. Romney has stated that China is "artificially holding down their prices" in an effort to weaken the U.S. economy. He has leveled complaints of **cyber espionage** against China. He claims that China regularly hacks into U.S. computer systems to steal valuable research and economic information. Romney has said that as president, he would apply taxes to Chinese imports to preserve American jobs. At the same time, he wants to

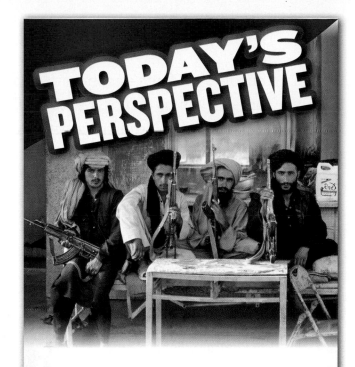

TODAY'S PERSPECTIVE

After the terrorist attacks of September 11, 2001, President George W. Bush's immediate priority became overthrowing Afghanistan's Taliban leadership. The Taliban is a militant group of Islamic **extremists**. It had ruled much of Afghanistan from 1996 to 2001 and had close ties to other terrorists. Though ousted from power by Bush's Operation Enduring Freedom, the Taliban continued to attack security forces in the region. A 2010 U.S. troop surge ordered by President Obama weakened Taliban resistance at first, but the organization has since grown in power.

encourage China's economic development and growth because China can be a strong ally in Afghanistan.

President Obama points to a gradually diminishing U.S. involvement in Afghanistan as a goal for his second term. With terrorist groups weakened, he hopes to turn over defense of Afghanistan to its military by 2014. Reflecting on the cost of the war, he said, "It is time to focus on nation building here at home."

Rising gas prices have led many Americans to become concerned about the nation's dependence on oil as a fuel source.

The Elephant in the Room

President Obama is concerned about America's dependence on oil. To reduce this dependence, he has proposed investing $150 billion over the next decade to develop renewable energy technologies. These would include wind and solar power. He has also encouraged U.S. automakers to increase hybrid vehicle production to lessen the country's dependence on oil.

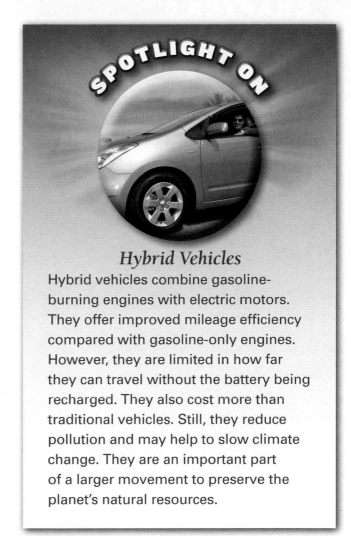

SPOTLIGHT ON

Hybrid Vehicles

Hybrid vehicles combine gasoline-burning engines with electric motors. They offer improved mileage efficiency compared with gasoline-only engines. However, they are limited in how far they can travel without the battery being recharged. They also cost more than traditional vehicles. Still, they reduce pollution and may help to slow climate change. They are an important part of a larger movement to preserve the planet's natural resources.

Romney believes in research and development for alternate energy sources as well, and is a supporter of nuclear energy. He has expressed an interest in expanding offshore drilling to decrease dependence on foreign oil, a plan that alarms environmentalists. Offshore drilling can sometimes lead to dangerous oil spills in the ocean. Oil spills cause major damage to plant and animal species living nearby.

CHAPTER 6

PAST AND FUTURE

Previous presidents, including Franklin D. Roosevelt, have had to deal with major crises during their terms in office.

THE 2012 ELECTION TAKES on added significance because of the many challenges facing the nation now and the ones that will occur in the future. While every presidential election is important for shaping the future, the choice facing voters this November brings to mind past elections. Some earlier presidents came to office when the country was struggling with problems that had begun years before. Other presidents were faced with unforeseen crises that required strong leadership.

Unemployment and poverty shook the nation during the Great Depression.

Dealing with the Depression

When Franklin Delano Roosevelt won the 1932 election, the Great Depression had been underway for more than three years. Unemployment stood at 25 percent, construction had come to a halt, and personal income had plummeted. The Great Depression, which had begun in the United States, ruined economies around the globe. Roosevelt's New Deal initiatives increased government spending and started several new agencies that created jobs. Roosevelt also established minimum wages, created the Social Security program, and supported unions. These changes have all had a positive effect on the economy.

The winner of the 2012 election will also have to deal with economic troubles. When voters go to the polls on November 6, they must choose the man they believe will help them recover from the hardships created by the recession.

Trouble Abroad

Soviet premier Nikita Khrushchev tested President John F. Kennedy's power by threatening an attack on West Berlin, Germany, in the summer of 1961. This was just months after Kennedy's inauguration. Tensions came to a head slightly more than a year later. Kennedy

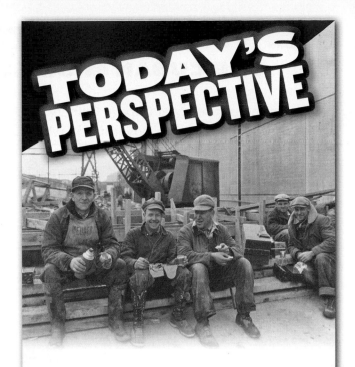

TODAY'S PERSPECTIVE

President Franklin Roosevelt's New Deal was set in place between 1933 and 1939. It tripled government spending to aid economic recovery, pay for public works projects, and fund Social Security. Roosevelt's critics were alarmed. They feared that the United States was getting away from the principles of government outlined in the Constitution.

Today, the debate continues over the extent to which government should intervene in the economy. Political conservatives distrusted President Obama's stimulus plans in part because of the political division that had occurred as a result the New Deal in the 1930s. The decisions a president makes continue to shape the political landscape for years.

A FIRSTHAND LOOK AT
THE CUBAN MISSILE CRISIS

Photographs taken over Cuba in October 1962 provided clear evidence that the Cuban government, which was politically aligned with the Soviet Union, was preparing nuclear missiles. Perhaps at no other time during the Cold War was the United States so close to getting involved in a nuclear war. See page 60 for a link to view these photographs online.

learned in October 1962 that the Soviets had been building up nuclear weapons in Cuba, less than 100 miles (161 kilometers) from the U.S. mainland. Kennedy's leadership helped the United States avoid nuclear war. What crises could the winner of the 2012 election face?

Many voters are still reeling from the effects of long, expensive wars in Iraq and Afghanistan. They will vote for a president with a foreign policy in line with their own beliefs. The rise of North Korea and Iran as nuclear powers threatens U.S. security at home and abroad. Voters remember the September 11 terrorist attacks, which defined the presidency of George W. Bush less than a year after he was elected in 2000.

That election was also defined by the controversy over the election process itself. Al Gore, Bush's opponent, narrowly won the popular vote, but fell short of the 270 electoral votes required to become president. Many people believed that the votes were counted unfairly in some parts of the country. Others pointed out that the election highlighted the imperfections in the electoral system.

The challenges facing the United States this election

year are complex. The candidates' policies have little in common. If Democratic incumbent Barack Obama wins, existing policies may remain in place. If Republican challenger Mitt Romney wins, many policy changes will be considered. Voters must examine their choices carefully as they select the candidate who will lead the nation for the next four years.

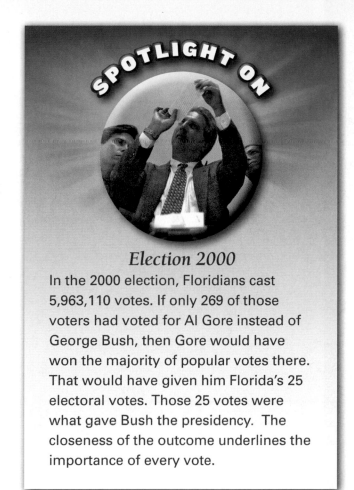

SPOTLIGHT ON

Election 2000

In the 2000 election, Floridians cast 5,963,110 votes. If only 269 of those voters had voted for Al Gore instead of George Bush, then Gore would have won the majority of popular votes there. That would have given him Florida's 25 electoral votes. Those 25 votes were what gave Bush the presidency. The closeness of the outcome underlines the importance of every vote.

If Mitt Romney wins the 2012 election, he will become the 45th president of the United States.

MAP OF THE EVENTS

What Happened Where?

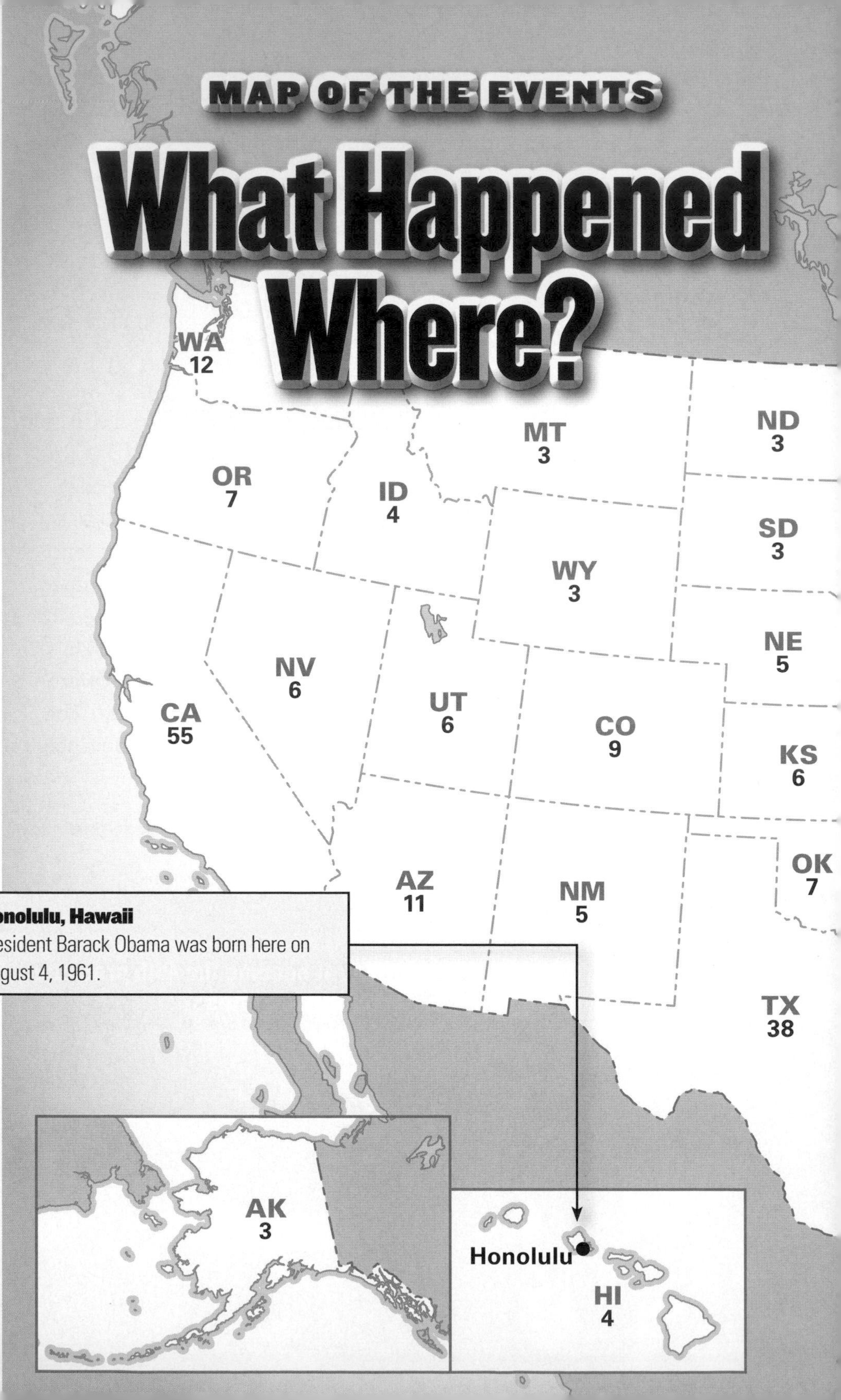

WA
12
OR
7
ID
4
MT
3
ND
3
SD
3
WY
3
NE
5
NV
6
UT
6
CO
9
KS
6
CA
55
AZ
11
NM
5
OK
7
TX
38
AK
3
Honolulu
HI
4

Honolulu, Hawaii
President Barack Obama was born here on August 4, 1961.

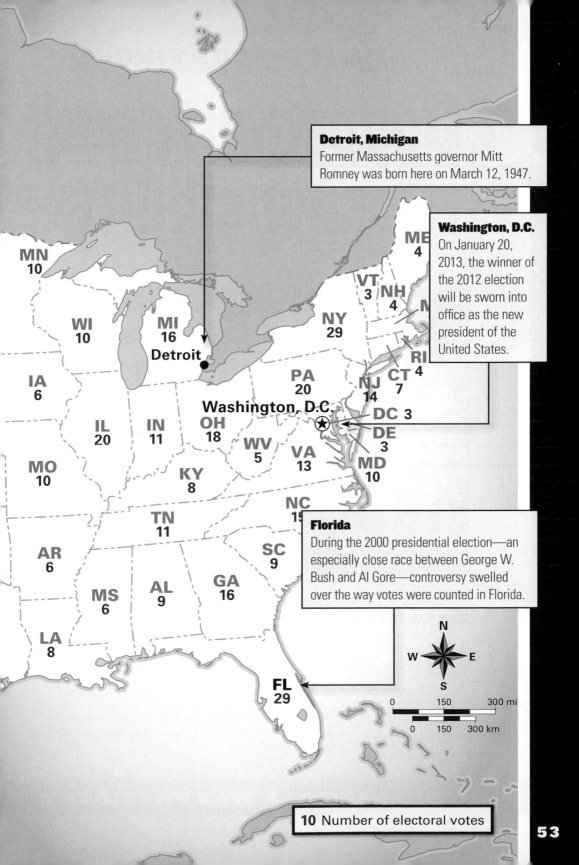

Detroit, Michigan
Former Massachusetts governor Mitt Romney was born here on March 12, 1947.

Washington, D.C.
On January 20, 2013, the winner of the 2012 election will be sworn into office as the new president of the United States.

Florida
During the 2000 presidential election—an especially close race between George W. Bush and Al Gore—controversy swelled over the way votes were counted in Florida.

MN 10
ME 4
VT 3
NH 4
WI 10
MI 16
NY 29
Detroit
IA 6
PA 20
RI 4
NJ 14
CT 7
IL 20
IN 11
OH 18
Washington, D.C.
DC 3
DE 3
MO 10
WV 5
VA 13
MD 10
KY 8
NC 15
TN 11
AR 6
SC 9
MS 6
AL 9
GA 16
LA 8
FL 29

N
W E
S

0   150   300 mi
0   150   300 km

10 Number of electoral votes

Opportunity and Responsibility

Protesters in Egypt forced longtime president Hosni Mubarak to step down from office in 2011.

We live in an age of protest and uncertainty. Beginning in 2010, major protests led to changes in the governments of Egypt, Tunisia, Yemen, and Libya. Large protest groups have also formed in the United States. The Tea Party gives

HOSNI MUBARAK WAS PRESIDENT

voice to the conservative beliefs held by some Americans. The Occupy movement speaks out against economic and social inequality that exists across the nation. Protesters have learned that their voices matter. They can influence the beliefs and behaviors of others.

Voters have the same power. Their goals are the same as those of the protesters. They want to do the most good for the most people when they cast their ballots. Voting is a serious responsibility. But it is also an opportunity. It is a chance to make the world a better place, to restore prosperity, and to save the planet. It is an opportunity and responsibility that will one day be yours.

Members of the Occupy movement believe that the U.S. government displays an unfair bias in favor of wealthy businesses and individuals.

OF EGYPT FROM 1981 UNTIL 2011.

Franklin D. Roosevelt

Franklin D. Roosevelt (1882–1945) was the 32nd president of the United States (1933–1945) and the architect of the New Deal. He also led the nation during World War II (1939–1945).

George Romney (1907–1995) served as president of American Motors (1954–1962), governor of Michigan (1963–1969), and secretary of Housing and Urban Development (1969–1973) under President Richard Nixon. He is the father of 2012 Republican presidential candidate Mitt Romney.

Lyndon Johnson (1908–1973) served as vice president under John F. Kennedy and later became the 36th president of the United States (1963–1969). Johnson increased U.S. involvement in the Vietnam War.

Lenore Romney (1908–1998) was the wife of George Romney and mother of presidential candidate Mitt Romney. She failed in her one attempt to win a U.S. Senate seat in 1970.

John F. Kennedy (1917–1963) was the 35th president of the United States (1961–1963). He averted nuclear war during the Cuban Missile Crisis, gave voice to America's aspirations in the Space Race, and started the Peace Corps.

Barack Obama Sr. (1936–1982) was a government economist from Kenya and the father of President Barack Obama.

Stanley Ann Dunham (1942–1995) was the mother of President Barack Obama. She was the future president's greatest influence during his youth.

Willard Mitt Romney (1947–) is the 2012 Republican presidential candidate. He holds a law degree and a master of business administration from Harvard University, and served as governor of Massachusetts (2003–2007). He was also a co-founder of Bain Capital and the leader of the organizing committee for the 2002 Salt Lake City Winter Olympics.

Mitt Romney

Ann Romney (1949–) is the wife of presidential candidate Mitt Romney and an active political campaigner. She is also active in children's charities.

Barack Obama (1961–) is the Nobel Peace Prize–winning 44th president of the United States. After graduating from Harvard Law School, he worked as a civil rights attorney and taught constitutional law at the University of Chicago Law School. He was elected to the Illinois State Senate in 1996 and the U.S. Senate in 2004.

Barack Obama

Michelle Robinson Obama (1964–) is the First Lady of the United States. A graduate of Harvard Law School, she now devotes herself to causes such as promoting healthy eating and supporting military families.

TIMELINE

1929–1941

The United States experiences the Great Depression.

1932

Franklin Roosevelt is elected president.

1933–1939

Roosevelt puts the New Deal in place.

1961

Nikita Khrushchev tests Kennedy's resolve.

August 4
Barack Obama is born in Honolulu, Hawaii.

1962

October
Cuban Missile Crisis unfolds.

1964

September
Lyndon Johnson's controversial "Daisy" advertisement airs.

2002

Mitt Romney leads the planning of the Salt Lake City Winter Olympics.

2003–2007

Romney serves one term as governor of Massachusetts.

2004

Obama becomes a U.S. senator from Illinois.

1941

The United States enters World War II.

1947

March 12
Willard Mitt Romney is born in Detroit, Michigan.

1960

November
John F. Kennedy is elected president.

1991

Barack Obama graduates from Harvard Law School.

2000

George W. Bush is elected president after a controversial, disputed election.

2001

The War in Afghanistan begins.

2008

Barack Obama is elected president.

2009, 2010

President Obama introduces his two economic stimulus packages.

2010

The Supreme Court's decision in *Citizens United v. Federal Election Commission* clears the way for super PACs.

LIVING HISTORY

Primary sources provide firsthand evidence about a topic. Witnesses to a historical event create primary sources. They include autobiographies, newspaper reports of the time, oral histories, photographs, and memoirs. A secondary source analyzes primary sources, and is one step or more removed from the event. Secondary sources include textbooks, encyclopedias, and commentaries. To view the following primary and secondary sources, go to www.factsfornow.scholastic.com. Enter the keywords **Election 2012** and look for the Living History logo ∑¡.

∑¡ **The American Recovery and Reinvestment Act** Visit this site to see how funds from the American Recovery and Reinvestment Act are being used.

∑¡ **The Cuban Missile Crisis** Photographs taken over Cuba in October 1962 provided clear evidence that the Cuban government was preparing nuclear missiles.

∑¡ **The Daisy Ad** On September 7, 1964, President Lyndon Johnson's reelection campaign aired an advertisement attacking opponent Barry Goldwater. It is considered one of the most extreme examples of negative campaigning.

∑¡ **A Democratic Campaign Video** A Democratic campaign video from early 2012 criticized Mitt Romney for speaking out against government bailouts after using them himself while leading the 2002 Salt Lake City Olympics Committee.

∑¡ **The Esfahan Nuclear Site** When reports of an explosion near the Esfahan Nuclear Site began to come out of Iran, investigators thought they might have their first substantial proof of an Iranian nuclear weapons program. Satellite images of the site are available online.

RESOURCES

Books

Abramson, Jill. *Obama: The Historic Journey*. New York: Callaway, 2009.

Heinrichs, Ann. *The Great Recession*. New York: Children's Press, 2012.

LeVert, Suzanne. *The Electoral College*. New York: Franklin Watts, 2004.

Rice, Earle. *FDR and the New Deal*. Hockessin, DE: Mitchell Lane Publishers, 2010.

Stein, R. Conrad. *Cuban Missile Crisis: In the Shadow of Nuclear War*. Berkeley Heights, NJ: Enslow Publishers, 2009.

Zeiger, Jennifer. *Barack Obama*. New York: Children's Press, 2012.

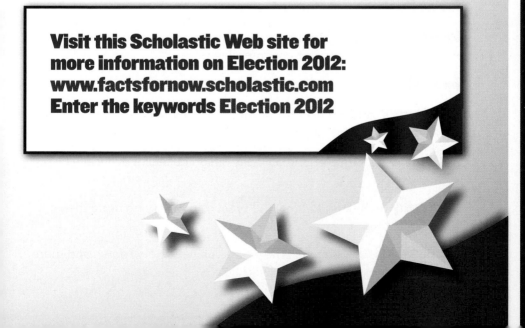

Visit this Scholastic Web site for more information on Election 2012: www.factsfornow.scholastic.com Enter the keywords Election 2012

GLOSSARY

apartheid (uh-PAR-tide) South Africa's former policy of racial segregation, officially ended in 1994

asbestos (as-BES-tuhs) a grayish mineral whose fibers can be woven into a fireproof fabric; it is rarely used today because breathing its fibers causes serious illness

conservative (kuhn-SUR-vuh-tiv) favoring smaller government and opposing large social welfare programs

cyber espionage (SYE-bur ES-pee-uh-nahzh) the use of computers to spy for a government or organization

economy (i-KAHN-uh-mee) the system of buying, selling, making things, and managing money in a place

extremists (ek-STREEM-ists) people who hold radical beliefs and refuse to compromise about certain issues

gubernatorial (goo-bur-nuh-TORE-ee-uhl) of or relating to the office of a state's governor

incumbent (in-KUHM-buhnt) currently in office

legislatures (LEJ-iss-lay-churz) government organizations that are responsible for making and changing laws

lobbied (LAH-beed) worked to influence lawmakers about a certain issue

missionary (MISH-uh-ner-ee) someone who travels to spread his or her religious faith among others

platforms (PLAT-formz) the officially stated beliefs of political candidates

polygamy (puh-LIH-guh-mee) the practice of marrying more than one person at a time

recession (ri-SESH-uhn) a time when business slows down and more workers than usual are unemployed

INDEX

Page numbers in *italics* indicate illustrations.

ABOUT THE AUTHOR

Peter Benoit is a graduate of Skidmore College in Saratoga Springs, New York. His degree is in mathematics. He is the author of dozens of Children's Press books, with topics as diverse as Native Americans, ecosystems, disasters, American history, and ancient civilizations. Peter has studied voting systems, the Electoral College, and election reform.